THE SPRING-COOKBOOK

50+ Delicious Recipes for the Spring

By
Chef Maggie Chow
Copyright © by Saxonberg Associates

Published by
BookSumo, a division of Saxonberg Associates
http://www.booksumo.com/

INTRODUCTION

Welcome to *The Effortless Chef Series*! Thank you for taking the time to download the *Easy Spring Cookbook*. Come take a journey with me into the delights of easy cooking. The point of this cookbook and all my cookbooks is to exemplify the effortless nature of cooking simply.

In this book we focus on springtime cooking. You will find that even though the recipes are simple, the taste of the dishes is quite amazing.

So will you join me in an adventure of simple cooking? If the answer is yes (and I hope it is) please consult the table of contents to find the dishes you are most interested in. Once you are ready jump right in and start cooking.

— Chef Maggie Chow

TABLE OF CONTENTS

ANY ISSUES? CONTACT ME

If you find that something important to you is missing from this book please contact me at maggie@booksumo.com.

I will try my best to re-publish a revised copy taking your feedback into consideration and let you know when the book has been revised with you in mind.

:)

— Chef Maggie Chow

LEGAL NOTES

COMMON ABBREVIATIONS

cup(s)	C.
tablespoon	tbsp
teaspoon	tsp
ounce	oz.
pound	lb

*All units used are standard American measurements

CHAPTER 1: EASY SPRING RECIPES

SOUTHERN BEEF AND BEAN SALAD

Ingredients

- 1 lb lean ground beef
- 2 tbsps chili powder
- 1/2 tsp ground cumin
- salt and pepper to taste
- 1 head iceberg lettuce, shredded
- 1 (15.5 oz.) can pinto beans
- 2 tomatoes, cubed
- 1 C. shredded Cheddar cheese
- 1/4 C. diced fresh cilantro
- 1 (12 oz.) package corn tortilla chips, broken
- 1 jalapeno pepper, seeded and diced (optional)
- 1/2 C. diced green onion (optional)
- 1 C. salsa (optional)

Directions

- Fry your beef until fully done then add in: pepper, chili powder, salt, and cumin.
- Get a bowl, combine: pinto beans with liquid, jalapenos, lettuce, salsa, cilantro, onions, tomatoes, and cheddar.
- Now add the corn chips and stir before adding the beef and mixing one more time.
- Enjoy.

Amount per serving (6 total)

Timing Information:

Preparation	15 m
Cooking	10 m
Total Time	25 m

Nutritional Information:

Calories	674 kcal
Fat	37.7 g
Carbohydrates	57.5g
Protein	29.5 g
Cholesterol	81 mg
Sodium	1043 mg

* Percent Daily Values are based on a 2,000 calorie diet.

TEX MEX SHRIMP

Ingredients

- 1 lb cooked medium shrimp, chilled
- 1/2 large cucumber, cut into 1/2 inch cubes
- 1/2 large tomato, cut into 1/2 inch cubes
- 8 green onions, thinly sliced
- 1 oz. fresh cilantro, finely diced
- 1 serrano pepper, thinly sliced
- 1 (8 oz.) can tomato sauce
- 2 tbsps white vinegar
- 1 lime

Directions

- Get a bowl, combine: vinegar, shrimp, tomato sauce, cucumber, serrano, green onions, and cilantro.
- Top this mix with the lime and place it in the fridge until chilled.
- Enjoy.

Amount per serving (8 total)

Timing Information:

Preparation	
Cooking	20 m
Total Time	20 m

Nutritional Information:

Calories	76 kcal
Fat	0.8 g
Carbohydrates	4.8g
Protein	12.9 g
Cholesterol	111 mg
Sodium	279 mg

* Percent Daily Values are based on a 2,000 calorie diet.

Oven Roasted Squash

Ingredients

- 1 lb ground beef
- 1/4 C. olive oil, divided
- 4 zucchini, cut into 1/2-inch cubes
- 1 red bell pepper, diced
- 1 jalapeno pepper, seeded and diced
- 4 cloves garlic, minced
- 4 green onions, diced -- white and green parts separated
- salt and pepper to taste
- 3 tbsps tomato paste
- 4 tsps chili powder, or to taste
- 2 tsps ground cumin, or to taste
- 1 (15 oz.) can black beans, rinsed and drained
- 1 (15 oz.) can kidney beans, rinsed and drained
- 1 C. frozen corn, thawed
- 1/2 C. grated Parmesan cheese, divided
- 1/4 C. diced fresh cilantro

Directions

- Stir fry your beef until fully done, for 10 mins, then break it into pieces.
- Now remove the meat from the pan.
- Coat a casserole dish with 1 tsp of olive oil and then set your oven to 400 degrees before doing anything else.
- Now add the rest of the oil to a pan and stir fry the following for 5 mins: green onions, zucchini, garlic, bell peppers, and jalapenos.

- Top the veggies with some pepper and salt. Then add: cumin, tomato paste, and chili powder.
- Let the contents gently boil for 60 secs then shut the heat.
- Add to the mix: a quarter of a C. of parmesan, ground beef, corn, kidney beans, and black beans.
- Pour the contents into the casserole dish and top everything with the rest of the parmesan.
- Place a covering of foil on the dish and cook everything in the oven for 27 mins.
- Now take off the foil and continue cooking for 5 more mins.
- Before serving, add a topping of cilantro.
- Enjoy.

Amount per serving (8 total)

Timing Information:

Preparation	30 m
Cooking	40 m
Total Time	1 h 10 m

Nutritional Information:

Calories	281 kcal
Fat	15.8 g
Carbohydrates	20g
Protein	17 g
Cholesterol	39 mg
Sodium	298 mg

* Percent Daily Values are based on a 2,000 calorie diet.

A Southern Style Potato Salad

Ingredients

- 1 (1 oz.) package ranch dressing mix
- 2 C. mayonnaise
- 3/4 C. diced green onion
- 1 lb bacon slices
- 5 lbs unpeeled red potatoes

Directions

- For 22 mins boil your potatoes in water and salt. Then remove the liquid and chunk the potatoes when cool.
- Place the chunks in a bowl and chill them in the fridge for 3 hrs.
- Get a 2nd bowl, combine: green onions, mayo, and ranch.
- Place a covering of plastic on this bowl, and place it in the fridge as well for 3 hours.
- For 17 mins microwave your bacon wrapped in paper towels.
- Once the bacon is cool, break it into pieces.
- Add the bacon to the mayo mix.
- Stir everything then add the mayo mix to the bowl with the potatoes.
- Stir everything again, then serve.
- Enjoy.

Amount per serving (16 total)

Timing Information:

Preparation	30 m
Cooking	30 m
Total Time	1 h

Nutritional Information:

Calories	353 kcal
Fat	25.9 g
Carbohydrates	24.8g
Protein	6.5 g
Cholesterol	21 mg
Sodium	503 mg

* Percent Daily Values are based on a 2,000 calorie diet.

TEXAS STYLE FRIED CHICKEN

Ingredients

- 2 C. buttermilk
- 1 tsp onion powder
- 1/4 C. diced fresh parsley
- 1/4 C. diced fresh tarragon
- 1/4 C. diced fresh sage
- 1 tsp paprika
- 1 tsp ground cayenne pepper
- 2 skinless, boneless chicken breast halves, halved
- 2 C. all-purpose flour
- 1 tsp garlic salt
- 1 tsp onion salt
- 1 tsp ground cayenne pepper
- salt and ground black pepper to taste
- 2 eggs
- 2 tbsps whole milk
- ground black pepper to taste
- 2 C. grapeseed oil for frying
- 1/2 C. all-purpose flour
- 1/2 C. quick-mixing flour (such as Wondra(R))
- 2 C. whole milk
- 1 pinch salt and ground white pepper to taste

Directions

- Get a bowl, combine: 1 tsp cayenne, buttermilk, paprika, onion powder, sage, parsley, and tarragon.
- Add in your chicken to the mix and coat the pieces evenly.
- Place a covering of plastic on the bowl and put everything in the fridge overnight.

- Get a 2nd bowl, mix: black pepper, 2 C. flour, salt, garlic salt, 1 tsp cayenne, and onion salt.
- Get a 3rd bowl, whisk: 2 tbsps milk, eggs, pepper, and salt.
- Get a 4rd bowl and add in 1/2 C. of flour without any spices.
- Dredge your chicken first in the 4th bowl, then the 3rd bowl, and finally the 2nd.
- For 10 mins, per side, fry your chicken in grapeseed oil then place on a rack.
- Leave a quarter of a C. of oil in the pan and begin adding the quick mix flour and milk to the oil while stirring.
- Get the mixing gently boiling and continue stirring until the gravy is thick.
- Now add some pepper and salt and top the chicken pieces with it.
- Enjoy.

Amount per serving (4 total)

Timing Information:

Preparation	30 m
Cooking	20 m
Total Time	8 h 50 m

Nutritional Information:

Calories	666 kcal
Fat	21.3 g
Carbohydrates	85.6g
Protein	32.7 g
Cholesterol	140 mg
Sodium	1151 mg

* Percent Daily Values are based on a 2,000 calorie diet.

ALMOND DIJON SALAD

Ingredients

- 1 C. sliced almonds
- 3 tbsps red wine vinegar
- 1/3 C. olive oil
- 1/4 C. fresh cranberries
- 1 tbsp Dijon mustard
- 1/2 tsp minced garlic
- 1/2 tsp salt
- 1/2 tsp ground black pepper
- 2 tbsps water
- 1/2 red onion, thinly sliced
- 4 oz. crumbled blue cheese
- 1 lb mixed salad greens

Directions

- Set your oven to 375 degrees before doing anything else.
- Place all your almonds on a cookie sheet and bake them for 7 mins in the oven
- Now puree the following with a food processor: water, vinegar, pepper, oil, salt, garlic, and mustard.
- Get a bowl, combine: the vinegar mix, baked almonds, greens, blue cheese, and onions.
- Enjoy.

Amount per serving (8 total)

Timing Information:

Preparation	15 m
Cooking	5 m
Total Time	20 m

Nutritional Information:

Calories	218 kcal
Fat	19.2 g
Carbohydrates	6.2g
Protein	6.5 g
Cholesterol	11 mg
Sodium	405 mg

* Percent Daily Values are based on a 2,000 calorie diet.

SEATTLE SALAD

Ingredients

- 1/2 C. freshly squeezed lemon juice
- 1/4 C. extra-virgin olive oil
- 2 tsps Dijon mustard
- salt and ground black pepper to taste
- 5 C. water
- 2 C. uncooked wild rice
- 1 tsp butter
- 4 C. finely sliced red cabbage
- 2 large red bell peppers - seeded, cored, and diced
- 2 bulbs fennel, trimmed and diced
- 2 bunches kale, leaves stripped from stems and torn into pieces
- 1/4 lemon, juiced, or to taste

Directions

- Get a bowl, combine: pepper, half C. lemon juice, Dijon, olive oil, and salt.
- Now get your wild rice boiling in water. Once it is boiling add the butter, place a lid on the pot, set the heat to low, and let the rice gently cook for 40 mins.
- Now remove any liquids and cook everything for 7 more mins until no liquid remains. Let the rice lose its heat then stir it.
- Get a 2nd bowl, combine: dressing, cabbage, fennel, and bell peppers.
- Lay your kale on top then add the wild rice over the kale.
- Let the salad sit for 7 mins before stirring.
- Now add some extra lemon juice then serve. Enjoy.

Amount per serving (12 total)

Timing Information:

Preparation	15 m
Cooking	35 m
Total Time	1 h

Nutritional Information:

Calories	211 kcal
Fat	6 g
Carbohydrates	35.2g
Protein	7.6 g
Cholesterol	< 1 mg
Sodium	< 103 mg

* Percent Daily Values are based on a 2,000 calorie diet.

AMERICAN POTATO SALAD

Ingredients

- 5 potatoes
- 3 eggs
- 1 C. diced celery
- 1/2 C. diced onion
- 1/2 C. sweet pickle relish
- 1/4 tsp garlic salt
- 1/4 tsp celery salt
- 1 tbsp prepared mustard
- ground black pepper to taste
- 1/4 C. mayonnaise

Directions

- Boil your potatoes in water and salt for 20 mins. Then remove the skins and chunk them.
- Now get your eggs boiling in water.
- Once the water is boiling, place a lid on the pot, and shut the heat.
- Let the eggs sit for 15 mins. Then once they have cooled remove the shells, and dice them.
- Get a bowl, combine: mayo, potatoes, pepper, eggs, mustard, celery, celery salt, onions, garlic, and relish.
- Place a covering of plastic on the mix and put everything in the fridge until it is cold.
- Enjoy.

Amount per serving (8 total)

Timing Information:

Preparation	45 m
Cooking	15 m
Total Time	1 h

Nutritional Information:

Calories	206 kcal
Fat	7.6 g
Carbohydrates	30.5g
Protein	5.5 g
Cholesterol	72 mg
Sodium	335 mg

* Percent Daily Values are based on a 2,000 calorie diet.

Tarragon Wild Rice Salad

Ingredients

- 1 1/2 C. uncooked wild rice
- 6 C. water
- 1/3 C. tarragon vinegar
- 3 tbsps Dijon mustard
- 1 tbsp white sugar
- 1 tsp salt
- 1 clove garlic, minced
- 1 tsp dried tarragon, crumbled
- 1/2 tsp black pepper
- 1/2 tsp crushed red pepper flakes
- 2/3 C. safflower oil
- 3 C. cubed cooked chicken
- 1 C. sliced celery
- 1/2 C. diced fresh parsley
- 1/2 C. sliced green onion
- 1/2 lb sugar snap peas, strings removed
- 1/2 C. toasted slivered almonds

Directions

- Get your rice boiling in water, place a lid on the pot, set the heat to low, and let the rice cook for 35 mins.
- Remove any extra liquids, and stir the rice.
- Let the rice continue to cook for 7 more mins to remove all the liquids. Then add the rice to a bowl.
- Get a 2nd bowl, combine: pepper flakes, vinegar, black pepper, mustard, tarragon, sugar, garlic, and salt.
- Add the safflower oil and whisk the contents until everything is smooth.

- Now add the following to your rice: green onions, chicken, parsley, and celery.
- Add in the wet oil mix then stir everything.
- Place a covering of plastic over the mix and put everything in the fridge for 5 hrs.
- Now begin to boil your peas in water and salt for 1 min.
- Remove the liquids and run them under cold water. Once the peas are chilled slice them diagonally.
- Combine the almonds and the peas with the rice mix and stir the contents evenly then serve the salad.
- Enjoy.

Amount per serving (10 total)

Timing Information:

Preparation	25 m
Cooking	20 m
Total Time	5 h 15 m

Nutritional Information:

Calories	326 kcal
Fat	20.7 g
Carbohydrates	19.2g
Protein	15.9 g
Cholesterol	32 mg
Sodium	390 mg

* Percent Daily Values are based on a 2,000 calorie diet.

QUINOA PEPPER SALAD

Ingredients

- 1 tsp canola oil
- 1 tbsp minced garlic
- 1/4 C. diced (yellow or purple) onion
- 2 1/2 C. water
- 2 tsps salt, or to taste
- 1/4 tsp ground black pepper
- 2 C. quinoa
- 3/4 C. diced fresh tomato
- 3/4 C. diced carrots
- 1/2 C. diced yellow bell pepper
- 1/2 C. diced cucumber
- 1/2 C. frozen corn kernels, thawed
- 1/4 C. diced red onion
- 1 1/2 tbsps diced fresh cilantro
- 1 tbsp diced fresh mint
- 1 tsp salt
- 1/4 tsp ground black pepper
- 2 tbsps olive oil
- 3 tbsps balsamic vinegar

Directions

- Stir fry 1/4 C. of onions and garlic in canola for 7 mins. Then add in: 1/4 tsp black pepper, water, 2 tsps salt.
- Get everything boiling then add in the quinoa.
- Place a lid on the pot, set the heat to low, and let the quinoa cook for 22 mins.
- Remove any excess liquids, place the mix in a bowl, and put everything in the fridge until it is cold, with a covering of plastic.

- Once the quinoa is cooled combine it with the following: 1/4 tsp black pepper, 1/4 C. red onions, 1 tsp salt, tomato, mint, corn, cilantro, carrots, cucumber, and bell peppers.
- Top the mix with balsamic and olive oil then stir the contents evenly.
- Enjoy.

Amount per serving (12 total)

Timing Information:

Preparation	20 m
Cooking	25 m
Total Time	1 h 30 m

Nutritional Information:

Calories	148 kcal
Fat	4.5 g
Carbohydrates	22.9g
Protein	4.6 g
Cholesterol	0 mg
Sodium	592 mg

* Percent Daily Values are based on a 2,000 calorie diet.

ASPARAGUS SALAD

Ingredients

- 1 lb fresh green beans, trimmed and cut into bite-size pieces
- 1 tbsp extra-virgin olive oil
- 1 lb fresh asparagus, trimmed and cut into bite-size pieces
- 1 tbsp extra-virgin olive oil
- 1/2 red onion, diced
- 2 C. cherry tomatoes, halved
- 1/4 C. diced fresh parsley
- kosher salt to taste
- ground black pepper to taste

Directions

- Set your oven to 400 degrees before doing anything else.
- Get a bowl, combine: olive oil (1 tbsp) and green beans.
- Layer the beans onto a cookie sheet and bake everything in the oven for 12 mins.
- Now combine your asparagus with 1 tbsp of olive oil, in the same bowl, then layer them on the same cookie sheet with the green beans.
- Cook the asparagus and beans for 12 more mins.
- Now in the same bowl, combine: parsley, black pepper, green beans, cherry tomatoes, kosher salt, asparagus, and red onions.
- Enjoy.

Amount per serving (8 total)

Timing Information:

Preparation	15 m
Cooking	20 m
Total Time	35 m

Nutritional Information:

Calories	71 kcal
Fat	3.7 g
Carbohydrates	8.8g
Protein	2.7 g
Cholesterol	0 mg
Sodium	59 mg

* Percent Daily Values are based on a 2,000 calorie diet.

RANCH PASTA SALAD

Ingredients

- 1 (12 oz.) package uncooked tri-color rotini pasta
- 10 slices bacon
- 1 C. mayonnaise
- 3 tbsps dry ranch salad dressing mix
- 1/4 tsp garlic powder
- 1/2 tsp garlic pepper
- 1/2 C. milk, or as needed
- 1 large tomato, diced
- 1 (4.25 oz.) can sliced black olives
- 1 C. shredded sharp Cheddar cheese

Directions

- Boil your pasta in water and salt for 9 mins, then remove the liquids.
- Stir fry your bacon then break it into pieces once it becomes crispy.
- Get a bowl, combine: garlic pepper, mayo, garlic powder, ranch dressing mix, and milk.
- Stir the contents then add in: cheese, rotini, black olives, bacon, and tomatoes.
- Stir the contents again until everything is smooth then place a covering of plastic around the bowl and put everything in the fridge for 65 mins.
- If the salad is too dry add a bit more milk, if needed.
- Enjoy.

Amount per serving (10 total)

Timing Information:

Preparation	10 m
Cooking	15 m
Total Time	1 h 25 m

Nutritional Information:

Calories	336 kcal
Fat	26.8 g
Carbohydrates	14.9g
Protein	9.3 g
Cholesterol	31 mg
Sodium	691 mg

* Percent Daily Values are based on a 2,000 calorie diet.

STRAWBERRY SESAME SALAD

Ingredients

- 2 tbsps sesame seeds
- 1 tbsp poppy seeds
- 1/2 C. white sugar
- 1/2 C. olive oil
- 1/4 C. distilled white vinegar
- 1/4 tsp paprika
- 1/4 tsp Worcestershire sauce
- 1 tbsp minced onion
- 10 oz. fresh spinach - rinsed, dried and torn into bite-size pieces
- 1 quart strawberries - cleaned, hulled and sliced
- 1/4 C. almonds, blanched and slivered

Directions

- Get a bowl, combine: onion, sesame seeds, Worcestershire, poppy seeds, paprika, sugar, vinegar, and olive oil.
- Place a covering of plastic around the bowl, and put everything in the fridge for 65 mins.
- Get a 2nd bowl, combine: almonds, spinach, and strawberries.
- Combine both bowls and place the combined mix in the fridge for 20 mins.
- Enjoy.

Amount per serving (4 total)

Timing Information:

Preparation	
Cooking	10 m
Total Time	1 h 10 m

Nutritional Information:

Calories	491 kcal
Fat	35.2 g
Carbohydrates	42.9g
Protein	6 g
Cholesterol	0 mg
Sodium	63 mg

* Percent Daily Values are based on a 2,000 calorie diet.

MEDITERRANEAN SALAD

Ingredients

- 3 cucumbers, seeded and sliced
- 1 1/2 C. crumbled feta cheese
- 1 C. black olives, pitted and sliced
- 3 C. diced roma tomatoes
- 1/3 C. diced oil packed sun-dried tomatoes, drained, oil reserved
- 1/2 red onion, sliced

Directions

- Get a bowl, combine: 2 tbsps sun dried tomato oil, red onions, cucumbers, sundried tomatoes, feta, roma tomatoes, and olives.
- Place a covering of plastic around the bowl and put everything in the fridge until it is cold.
- Enjoy.

Amount per serving (8 total)

Timing Information:

Preparation	
Cooking	10 m
Total Time	10 m

Nutritional Information:

Calories	131 kcal
Fat	8.8 g
Carbohydrates	9.3g
Protein	5.5 g
Cholesterol	25 mg
Sodium	486 mg

* Percent Daily Values are based on a 2,000 calorie diet.

CRANBERRY SALAD

Ingredients

- 1 tbsp butter
- 3/4 C. almonds, blanched and slivered
- 1 lb spinach, rinsed and torn into bite-size pieces
- 1 C. dried cranberries
- 2 tbsps toasted sesame seeds
- 1 tbsp poppy seeds
- 1/2 C. white sugar
- 2 tsps minced onion
- 1/4 tsp paprika
- 1/4 C. white wine vinegar
- 1/4 C. cider vinegar
- 1/2 C. vegetable oil

Directions

- Toast your almonds in butter for 7 mins then place them to the side.
- Get a bowl, combine: veggie oil, sesame seeds, cider vinegar, poppy seeds, wine vinegar, sugar, paprika, and onions.
- Combine in the cranberries, almonds, and spinach and toss the contents.
- Enjoy.

Amount per serving (8 total)

Timing Information:

Preparation	10 m
Cooking	10 m
Total Time	20 m

Nutritional Information:

Calories	338 kcal
Fat	23.5 g
Carbohydrates	30.4g
Protein	4.9 g
Cholesterol	4 mg
Sodium	58 mg

* Percent Daily Values are based on a 2,000 calorie diet.

ASIAN STYLE BROCCOLI AND CHICKEN

Ingredients

- 3 C. broccoli florets
- 1 tbsp olive oil
- 2 skinless, boneless chicken breast halves - cut into 1 inch strips
- 1/4 C. sliced green onions
- 4 cloves garlic, thinly sliced
- 1 tbsp hoisin sauce
- 1 tbsp chili paste
- 1 tbsp low sodium soy sauce
- 1/2 tsp ground ginger
- 1/4 tsp crushed red pepper
- 1/2 tsp salt
- 1/2 tsp black pepper
- 1/8 C. chicken stock

Directions

- With a steamer insert and 2 inches of water steam your broccoli for 6 mins.
- Now stir fry: garlic, chicken, and green onions until the chicken is fully done.
- Add in with the chicken the following: chicken stock, soy sauce, black pepper, ginger, salt, red pepper, chili paste, and hoisin.
- Get the broth boiling and let it continue boiling for 4 mins. Now add in your broccoli and let it cook until the sauce thickens for about 1 more min.
- Enjoy with jasmine rice.

Amount per serving (4 total)

Timing Information:

Preparation	Cooking	Total Time
10 m	20 m	30 m

Nutritional Information:

Calories	156 kcal
Fat	6.2 g
Carbohydrates	10.9g
Protein	15.9 g
Cholesterol	36 mg
Sodium	606 mg

* Percent Daily Values are based on a 2,000 calorie diet.

Broccoli Salad IV (Peanuts and Ramen)

Ingredients

- 1 (16 oz.) package broccoli coleslaw mix
- 2 (3 oz.) packages chicken flavored ramen noodles
- 1 bunch green onions, chopped
- 1 C. unsalted peanuts
- 1 C. sunflower seeds
- 1/2 C. white sugar
- 1/4 C. vegetable oil
- 1/3 C. cider vinegar

Directions

- Get a bowl, mix: green onions, vinegar, sugar, crushed ramen and its seasoning, oil, and slaw.
- Toss the slaw mix and then add seeds and peanuts.
- Enjoy chilled after 20 mins in the fridge.

Amount per serving (6 total)

Timing Information:

Preparation	Cooking	Total Time
15 m		45 m

Nutritional Information:

Calories	562 kcal
Fat	34.4 g
Carbohydrates	52.3g
Protein	16.5 g
Cholesterol	0 mg
Sodium	356 mg

* Percent Daily Values are based on a 2,000 calorie diet.

Honey Mustard Chicken and Broccoli

Ingredients

- 2 C. chopped, cooked chicken meat
- 2 C. fresh chopped broccoli
- 1/2 C. chopped onion
- 2 tbsps honey
- 1/2 C. chopped green bell pepper
- 1 1/2 C. shredded Cheddar cheese
- 1/2 C. mayonnaise
- 2 tbsps Dijon-style prepared mustard
- salt and pepper to taste
- 1 tbsp minced garlic
- 1 (8 oz.) package refrigerated crescent rolls

Directions

- Set your oven to 400 degrees before doing anything else.
- Get a bowl, mix: garlic, chicken, pepper, broccoli, salt, honey, onions, mustard, bell peppers, mayo, and cheese. Line a baking dish or casserole dish with foil. Get a 2nd bowl and place it upside down on the dish and roll out your dough around the top of the bowl.
- Add some chicken to the rolled out dough and fold to form a roll around the mix. Repeat for any remaining dough or mixture.
- Place the roll on the sheet and cook in the oven for 27 mins.
- Enjoy.

Amount per serving (16 total)

Timing Information:

Preparation	Cooking	Total Time
10 m	30 m	40 m

Nutritional Information:

Calories	183 kcal
Fat	12.7 g
Carbohydrates	7.8g
Protein	8.9 g
Cholesterol	27 mg
Sodium	275 mg

* Percent Daily Values are based on a 2,000 calorie diet.

ASIAN STYLE BROCCOLI AND BEEF II

Ingredients

- 2 tbsps low-sodium soy sauce
- 2 tbsps fat-free Italian dressing
- 1 tsp cornstarch
- 1 tbsp minced garlic
- 1 tsp ground ginger
- 3/4 lb round steak, cut into strips
- 6 C. water
- 5 cubes beef bouillon
- 4 oz. linguine pasta, uncooked
- 1/2 C. fat free beef broth
- 1 C. fresh mushrooms, sliced
- 1/2 C. sliced green onion
- 1 lb broccoli, separated into florets

Directions

- Get a bowl, combine: ginger, soy sauce, garlic, steak, cornstarch, and dressing.
- Cover the bowl with plastic wrap and place it in the fridge for 20 mins.
- Simultaneously while the steak is soaking boil your pasta in water and bouillon for 9 mins. The remove the excess liquid. Stir fry your beef for 3 mins until browned and cooked through and add in the broth, onions, and mushrooms. Get the broth boiling and then place a lid on the pan and let the contents lightly boil for 7 mins. Take off the lid and input your broccoli and stir the mix until you find that the broccoli is a bit soft and bright in colour.
- Finally combine the beef and sauce with the pasta and stir to evenly coat.
- Enjoy.

Amount per serving (4 total)

Timing Information:

Preparation	Cooking	Total Time
15 m	45 m	1 h

Nutritional Information:

Calories	303 kcal
Fat	7.1 g
Carbohydrates	35.1g
Protein	26.4 g
Cholesterol	46 mg
Sodium	1533 mg

* Percent Daily Values are based on a 2,000 calorie diet.

Broccoli Salad V

(Bacon, Tomatoes, and Tortellini)

Ingredients

- 2 (9 oz.) packages refrigerated three-cheese tortellini
- 1 lb bacon
- 4 C. chopped broccoli
- 1 pint grape tomatoes, halved
- 2 green onions, finely chopped
- 1 C. bottled coleslaw dressing

Directions

- Boil your pasta in water and salt for about 8 mins then remove all the liquid and place the pasta in the fridge and in a bowl for 35 mins.
- Fry your bacon for 9 to 12 mins, remove excess oils and then place the bacon on paper towels. Now break it into pieces after a good amount of grease has been absorbed by the towels.
- Get a big bowl, toss: green onions, pasta, tomatoes, dressing, broccoli, and bacon.
- Place the mix in the fridge for 10 to 20 min until fully chilled then serve.
- Enjoy.

Amount per serving (10 total)

Timing Information:

Preparation	Cooking	Total Time
15 m	15 m	1 h 30 m

Nutritional Information:

Calories	349 kcal
Fat	18.2 g
Carbohydrates	33.6g
Protein	13.9 g
Cholesterol	47 mg
Sodium	736 mg

* Percent Daily Values are based on a 2,000 calorie diet.

JALAPENOS, PEAS, AND MINT COUSCOUS

Ingredients

- 2 C. dry couscous
- 1/2 C. chopped green onions
- 1 fresh jalapeno pepper, finely diced
- 2 tbsps olive oil
- 1/2 tsp ground cumin
- 1 pinch cayenne pepper
- 1 pinch ground black pepper
- 2 C. vegetable stock
- 1 bunch asparagus, trimmed and cut into 1/4-inch pieces
- 1 C. shelled fresh or thawed frozen peas
- 2 tbsps chopped fresh mint
- salt and freshly ground black pepper to taste

Directions

- Get a bowl, mix: black pepper, couscous, cayenne, onions, cumin, olive oil, and jalapenos.
- Get your peas and asparagus boiling in the veggie stock and then pour it into the bowl.
- Stir the couscous into the liquid and place a covering on the bowl.
- Let the mix sit for 12 mins then stir it.
- Add some mint, pepper, and salt before serving.
- Enjoy.

Amount per serving (6 total)

Timing Information:

Preparation	Cooking	Total Time
15 m	20 m	35 m

Nutritional Information:

Calories	306 kcal
Fat	5.3 g
Carbohydrates	53.7g
Protein	10.9 g
Cholesterol	0 mg
Sodium	228 mg

* Percent Daily Values are based on a 2,000 calorie diet.

CHICKEN, CUCUMBERS, AND PARSLEY COUSCOUS

Ingredients

- 2 C. chicken broth
- 1 (10 oz.) box couscous
- 3/4 C. olive oil
- 1/4 C. fresh lemon juice
- 2 tbsps white balsamic vinegar
- 1/4 C. chopped fresh rosemary leaves
- salt and ground black pepper to taste
- 2 large cooked skinless, boneless chicken breast halves, cut into bite-size pieces

- 1 C. chopped English cucumber
- 1/2 C. chopped sun-dried tomatoes
- 1/2 C. chopped pitted kalamata olives
- 1/2 C. crumbled feta cheese
- 1/3 C. chopped fresh Italian parsley
- salt and ground black pepper to taste

Directions

- Get your stock boiling then add in your couscous.
- Place a lid on the pot and shut the heat.
- Let the contents sit for 7 mins before stirring.
- Blend: vinegar, olive oil, and lemon juice with some rosemary.

- Now add some pepper and salt before continuing.
- Get a bowl, mix: tomatoes, parsley, couscous, feta, cucumbers, and chicken.
- Cover the couscous with the dressing and add a bit more if you like also add some more pepper and salt too.
- Enjoy.

Amount per serving (6 total)

Timing Information:

Preparation	Cooking	Total Time
35 m	10 m	45 m

Nutritional Information:

Calories	645 kcal
Fat	38.8 g
Carbohydrates	44g
Protein	29.4 g
Cholesterol	68 mg
Sodium	792 mg

* Percent Daily Values are based on a 2,000 calorie diet.

LIME AND CHICKEN COUSCOUS

Ingredients

- 1 tbsp olive oil
- 1 lb skinless, boneless chicken breast halves, cubed
- 1 pinch monosodium glutamate (MSG)
- 6 tbsps soy sauce
- 6 tbsps brown sugar
- 1/2 tsp red pepper flakes, or more to taste
- 1 lime, juiced and zested
- 2 C. vegetable broth
- 1 C. couscous
- 1/3 C. chopped cilantro
- 4 wedges lime for garnish

Directions

- Get a bowl, combine: zest, soy sauce, lime juice, sugar, and pepper flakes.
- Boil everything gently for 4 mins until it becomes sauce like.
- Now stir fry your chicken until it is fully done in olive oil for 7 mins.
- Add in your MSG while it fries.
- Then top everything with the lime sauce and continue stir frying for 4 more mins.
- Let your couscous sit in the veggie broth that was boiling for 7 mins in a covered pot.
- Place some couscous on a plate for serving and add a topping of lime chicken.
- Garnish with freshly squeezed lime from the wedges.
- Enjoy.

Amount per serving (4 total)

Timing Information:

Preparation	Cooking	Total Time
15 m	15 m	35 m

Nutritional Information:

Calories	380 kcal
Fat	6.2 g
Carbohydrates	52g
Protein	28.4 g
Cholesterol	59 mg
Sodium	1675 mg

* Percent Daily Values are based on a 2,000 calorie diet.

Peppers, Corn, and Black Beans Couscous

Ingredients

- 1 C. uncooked couscous
- 1 1/4 C. chicken broth
- 3 tbsps extra virgin olive oil
- 2 tbsps fresh lime juice
- 1 tsp red wine vinegar
- 1/2 tsp ground cumin
- 8 green onions, chopped
- 1 red bell pepper, seeded and chopped
- 1/4 C. chopped fresh cilantro
- 1 C. frozen corn kernels, thawed
- 2 (15 oz.) cans black beans, drained
- salt and pepper to taste

Directions

- Get your broth boiling for 2 mins then add in your couscous.
- Place a lid on the pot and shut the heat.
- Let the couscous sit in the hot water for 7 mins, before stirring it.
- Get a bowl, mix: beans, olive oil, couscous, corn, lime juice, cilantro, vinegar, red pepper, onions, and cumin.
- Add your preferred amount of pepper and salt. Then place a plastic covering around the bowl, let the mix sit in the fridge for 20 to 30 mins before serving.
- Enjoy.

Amount per serving (8 total)

Timing Information:

Preparation	Cooking	Total Time
30 m		35 m

Nutritional Information:

Calories	255 kcal
Fat	5.9 g
Carbohydrates	41.2g
Protein	10.4 g
Cholesterol	< 1 mg
Sodium	565 mg

* Percent Daily Values are based on a 2,000 calorie diet.

CREAMY PARSLEY, CHICKPEAS, AND ALMONDS COUSCOUS

Ingredients

- 1/2 C. creamy salad dressing
- 1/4 C. plain yogurt
- 1 tsp ground cumin
- salt and pepper to taste
- 1 tbsp butter
- 1/2 C. couscous
- 1 C. water
- 1 red onion, chopped
- 1 red bell pepper, chopped
- 1/3 C. chopped parsley
- 1/3 C. raisins
- 1/3 C. toasted and sliced almonds
- 1/2 C. canned chickpeas, drained

Directions

- Get a bowl, combine: pepper, salad dressing, salt, cumin, and yogurt.
- Cover the bowl with some plastic wrap and chill in the fridge for 1 h.
- Simultaneously toast your couscous in butter for 2 mins then add your water.
- Get everything boiling, then place a lid on the pot, set the heat to low and let the contents gently boil for 7 mins. Get your dressing mix and add in: chickpeas, couscous, almonds, red onions, raisins, parsley, and bell peppers.
- Place the covering back on the bowl and put it back in the fridge for 20 mins.
- Enjoy.

Amount per serving (6 total)

Timing Information:

Preparation	Cooking	Total Time
15 m	30 m	1 h 45 m

Nutritional Information:

Calories	247 kcal
Fat	12.2 g
Carbohydrates	30g
Protein	5.7 g
Cholesterol	13 mg
Sodium	251 mg

* Percent Daily Values are based on a 2,000 calorie diet.

VEGGIE TURKEY COUSCOUS BITS COUSCOUS

Ingredients

- 2 C. coarsely chopped zucchini
- 1 1/2 C. coarsely chopped onions
- 1 red bell pepper, coarsely chopped
- 1 lb extra lean ground turkey
- 1/2 C. uncooked couscous
- 1 egg
- 2 tbsps Worcestershire sauce
- 1 tbsp Dijon mustard
- 1/2 C. barbecue sauce, or as needed

Directions

- Coat your muffin pan with non-stick spray and then set your oven to 400 degrees before doing anything else.
- Blend with a few pulses: bell peppers, zucchini, and onions. Then add them to a bowl, with: mustard, turkey, Worcestershire, eggs, and couscous.
- Evenly divide the mix between the sections in your muffin pan then add bbq sauce to each (1 tsp).
- Cook everything in the oven for 27 mins.
- Check the temperature of each, it should be 160 degrees.
- Let the dish sit for 10 mins before serving.
- Enjoy.

Amount per serving (10 total)

Timing Information:

Preparation	Cooking	Total Time
20 m	25 m	50 m

Nutritional Information:

Calories	119 kcal
Fat	1 g
Carbohydrates	13.6g
Protein	13.2 g
Cholesterol	47 mg
Sodium	244 mg

* Percent Daily Values are based on a 2,000 calorie diet.

Squash and Garbanzos Couscous
(Moroccan Style III)

Ingredients

- 2 tbsps brown sugar
- 1 tbsp butter, melted
- 2 large acorn squash, halved and seeded
- 2 tbsps olive oil
- 2 cloves garlic, chopped
- 2 stalks celery, chopped
- 2 carrots, chopped
- 1 C. garbanzo beans, drained
- 1/2 C. raisins
- 1 1/2 tbsps ground cumin
- salt and pepper to taste
- 1 (14 oz.) can chicken broth
- 1 C. uncooked couscous

Directions

- Set your oven to 350 degrees before doing anything else. Cook your squash for 32 mins in the oven. Then top the squash with a mix of butter and sugar that has been melted and stirred together. Stir fry, for 7 mins, in olive oil: carrots, celery, and garlic. Now add the raisins and beans. Fry the contents until everything is soft then add in pepper, salt, and cumin. Add the broth to the carrot mix and then add the couscous. Place a lid on the pot and place the pot to the side away from all heat. Let the contents sit for 7 mins.
- Fill your squashes with the couscous mix. Enjoy.

Amount per serving (4 total)

Timing Information:

Preparation	Cooking	Total Time
15 m	45 m	1 h

Nutritional Information:

Calories	502 kcal
Fat	11.7 g
Carbohydrates	93.8g
Protein	11.2 g
Cholesterol	10 mg
Sodium	728 mg

* Percent Daily Values are based on a 2,000 calorie diet.

CHERRY TOMATOES, ONIONS, AND BASIL COUSCOUS

Ingredients

- 1 C. couscous
- 1 C. boiling water
- 3 tbsps olive oil
- 1 clove garlic, minced
- 1/4 C. diced red bell pepper
- 4 green onions, sliced
- 1 C. cherry tomatoes
- 1 C. fresh basil leaves
- 1 pinch salt
- 1 pinch ground black pepper
- 1 dash balsamic vinegar
- 1/4 C. grated Parmesan cheese

Directions

- Set your oven to 350 degrees before doing anything else.
- Get your water boiling then pour in your couscous.
- Get everything boiling again. Then place a lid on the pot, shut the heat, and let the mix sit for 7 mins before stirring.
- Simultaneously stir fry your peppers, onions, and garlic for 3 mins then add: pepper, tomatoes, salt, basil, and couscous.
- Pour everything into a baking dish and add in your balsamic.
- Cook everything in the oven for 25 mins then add the parmesan.
- Enjoy.

Amount per serving (4 total)

Timing Information:

Preparation	Cooking	Total Time
5 m	35 m	40 m

Nutritional Information:

Calories	299 kcal
Fat	12.4 g
Carbohydrates	38g
Protein	9.1 g
Cholesterol	6 mg
Sodium	196 mg

* Percent Daily Values are based on a 2,000 calorie diet.

Mangos, and Salsa Couscous

Ingredients

- 1 1/2 C. water
- 1 C. couscous
- 2/3 C. dried mango, diced
- 3/4 C. prepared salsa
- 2 tsps ground cumin
- 1 tsp curry powder

Directions

- Get the following boiling in a big pot: curry, couscous, water, cumin, mango, and salsa.
- Place a lid on the pot and set the heat to low.
- Cook everything for 4 mins and then let the contents sit for 7 more mins. Stir the couscous before plating.
- Enjoy.

Amount per serving (4 total)

Timing Information:

Preparation	Cooking	Total Time
10 m	5 m	20 m

Nutritional Information:

Calories	186 kcal
Fat	0.9 g
Carbohydrates	40.2g
Protein	5.1 g
Cholesterol	0 mg
Sodium	314 mg

* Percent Daily Values are based on a 2,000 calorie diet.

Moroccan Salmon Cake

Ingredients

Mayo Topping:

- 1/2 C. mayonnaise
- 1 clove garlic, crushed
- 1/8 tsp paprika

Salmon Cake:

- 1/2 C. couscous
- 2/3 C. orange juice
- 1 (14.75 oz.) can red salmon, drained

- 1 (10 oz.) package frozen chopped spinach, thawed, drained and squeezed dry
- 2 egg yolks, beaten
- 2 cloves garlic, crushed
- 1 tsp ground cumin
- 1/2 tsp ground black pepper
- 1/2 tsp salt
- 3 tbsps olive oil

Directions

- Get a bowl, mix: paprika, mayo, and garlic.
- Boil your orange juice in a large pot, then add in your couscous.
- Get the mix boiling again and then place a lid on the pot, shut the heat, and let the couscous stand for 7 mins.
- Now stir your couscous after it has lost all of its heat.
- Get a 2nd bowl, combine: salt, salmon, black pepper, spinach, cumin, egg yolks, and garlic.

- Shape this mix into patties and then fry them in olive oil for 8 mins turning each at 4 mins.
- When serving add a topping of mayo.
- Enjoy.

Amount per serving (4 total)

Timing Information:

Preparation	Cooking	Total Time
20 m	25 m	45 m

Nutritional Information:

Calories	620 kcal
Fat	46.4 g
Carbohydrates	26.4g
Protein	28.8 g
Cholesterol	178 mg
Sodium	950 mg

* Percent Daily Values are based on a 2,000 calorie diet.

Feta, Balsamic, and Asparagus Couscous

Ingredients

- 2 C. couscous
- 1 bunch fresh asparagus, trimmed and cut into 2-inch pieces
- 8 oz. grape tomatoes, halved
- 6 oz. feta cheese, crumbled
- 3 tbsps balsamic vinegar
- 2 tbsps extra-virgin olive oil
- Black pepper, to taste

Directions

- Boil your couscous in water, then place a lid on the pot, shut the heat, and let the couscous sit for 7 mins.
- Once it has cooled stir it with a fork.
- Simultaneously steam your asparagus over 2 inches of boiling water with a steamer insert and a pot. Steam the spears for 7 mins. Now remove all the liquid.
- Get a bowl, toss: couscous, olive oil, asparagus, balsamic, cheese, pepper, and tomatoes.
- Enjoy chilled or warm.

Amount per serving (4 total)

Timing Information:

Preparation	Cooking	Total Time
10 m	20 m	30 m

Nutritional Information:

Calories	541 kcal
Fat	16.7 g
Carbohydrates	77.7g
Protein	20.1 g
Cholesterol	38 mg
Sodium	494 mg

* Percent Daily Values are based on a 2,000 calorie diet.

PEPPERS, CUCUMBERS, AND OLIVES COUSCOUS (GREEK STYLE II)

Ingredients

- 3 (6 oz.) packages garlic and herb couscous mix
- 1 pint cherry tomatoes, cut in half
- 1 (5 oz.) jar pitted kalamata olives, halved
- 1 C. mixed bell peppers (green, red, yellow, orange), diced
- 1 cucumber, sliced and then halved
- 1/2 C. parsley, finely chopped
- 1 (8 oz.) package crumbled feta cheese
- 1/2 C. Greek vinaigrette salad dressing

Directions

- Get your couscous boiling in water for 2 mins. Then place a lid on the pot, shut and heat, and it sit for 7 mins before stirring after it has cooled.
- Place the couscous in a bowl, and combine in: cheese, tomatoes, parsley, olives, cucumber, and bell peppers.
- Add in your Greek dressing and toss everything to coat evenly.
- Feel free to add more dressing if you like.
- Enjoy.

Amount per serving (20 total)

Timing Information:

Preparation	Cooking	Total Time
30 m	15 m	45 m

Nutritional Information:

Calories	159 kcal
Fat	6.5 g
Carbohydrates	21.4g
Protein	5.7 g
Cholesterol	10 mg
Sodium	642 mg

* Percent Daily Values are based on a 2,000 calorie diet.

CLOVES, ONIONS, TOMATOES, AND CHICKEN COUSCOUS (MOROCCAN STYLE IV)

Ingredients

- 1 C. whole wheat couscous
- 1 tbsp vegetable oil
- 1 medium onion, chopped
- 2 bay leaves
- 5 whole cloves, crushed
- 1/2 tsp cinnamon
- 1 tsp ground dried turmeric
- 1/4 tsp ground cayenne pepper
- 6 skinless, boneless chicken breast halves - chopped
- 1 (16 oz.) can garbanzo beans
- 1 (16 oz.) can crushed tomatoes
- 1 (48 fluid oz.) can chicken broth
- 2 carrots, cut into 1/2 inch pieces
- 1 zucchini, cut into 1/2-inch pieces
- salt to taste

Directions

- Get your couscous boiling in water for 2 mins. Then place a lid on the pot, shut and heat, and it sit for 7 mins before stirring once it has cooled.
- Stir fry your onions in oil until soft then add in: cayenne, bay leaves, turmeric, cloves, and cinnamon.
- Cook everything for 1 more min then pour in your chicken and cook it until browned all over.

- Once everything has been browned add in: broth, tomatoes, and beans.
- Get everything boiling.
- Lower the heat to low and gently boil for 27 mins.
- Now add your zucchini and carrots and also some salt.
- Continue for 12 more mins.
- Serve the veggies and chicken over the couscous.
- Enjoy.

Amount per serving (6 total)

Timing Information:

Preparation	Cooking	Total Time
15 m	45 m	1 h

Nutritional Information:

Calories	399 kcal
Fat	6.7 g
Carbohydrates	50.7g
Protein	33.4 g
Cholesterol	67 mg
Sodium	1539 mg

* Percent Daily Values are based on a 2,000 calorie diet.

Mozzarella, Tomato, Basil Panini

Ingredients

- 1 French deli roll, split
- 1 tsp balsamic vinegar
- 2 slices mozzarella cheese
- 1 small tomato, sliced
- 4 fresh basil leaves
- olive oil

Directions

- Heat up your skillet over medium heat.
- Spread some balsamic vinegar on a roll before putting mozzarella cheese, basil leaves, tomato slice and the remaining cheese on top of all this.
- Rub the outside with olive before heating it up on the skillet for about three minutes each side or until you see that it golden brown from the outside.
- Serve.

Serving: 1

Timing Information:

Preparation	Cooking	Total Time
10 mins	5 mins	15 mins

Nutritional Information:

Calories	402 kcal
Carbohydrates	29.9 g
Cholesterol	36 mg
Fat	24.1 g
Fiber	2.1 g
Protein	18.5 g
Sodium	613 mg

* Percent Daily Values are based on a 2,000 calorie diet.

Turkey, Sundried Tomato, Basil Panini

Ingredients

- 4 Dinner Rolls, split
- Plain or sundried tomato mayonnaise (see below)
- 4 slices roast turkey or ham
- 4 slices Swiss, Monterey Jack, or Gruyere cheese
- 8 small slices red onion
- 1 C. fresh spinach leaves or several fresh basil leaves(optional)
- Salt and freshly ground black pepper
- Butter

Tomato Mayo:

- 1/4 C. mayonnaise
- 2 finely chopped sundried tomatoes
- Salt and freshly ground black pepper

Directions

- Spread mayonnaise and place all the ingredients except over roll.
- Grill sandwich on the Panini machine for seven minutes (three minutes if you are using a pan) after spreading some butter on the top and bottom.
- Whisk all the ingredients for mayonnaise together and set it aside for later use.

Serving: 4

Timing Information:

Preparation	Cooking	Total Time
10 mins	10 mins	20 mins

Nutritional Information:

Calories	464 kcal
Carbohydrates	40.8 g
Cholesterol	60 mg
Fat	26.6 g
Fiber	3.8 g
Protein	17.4 g
Sodium	936 mg

* Percent Daily Values are based on a 2,000 calorie diet.

HUMMUS, EGGPLANT, MOZZARELLA PANINI

Ingredients

- 1 baby eggplant, cut into 1/4-inch slices
- salt and ground black pepper to taste
- 1/4 C. olive oil, divided
- 1 loaf flat bread, sliced horizontally and cut into 4 equal pieces
- 1/2 (12 oz) jar roasted red bell peppers, drained and sliced
- 4 oz shredded mozzarella cheese
- 1/4 C. roasted garlic hummus

Directions

- Coat eggplant slices with salt and pepper before letting it stand as it is for two minutes.
- Cook eggplant in batches in hot olive oil for about three minutes each side.
- Put eggplant, mozzarella cheese and red pepper over bread before spreading some hummus over the top piece of bread.
- Now grill these Paninis on a preheated Panini press for about 7 minutes or until the cheese has melted.

Serving: 1

Timing Information:

Preparation	Cooking	Total Time
15 mins	15 mins	30 mins

Nutritional Information:

Calories	401 kcal
Carbohydrates	41.5 g
Cholesterol	18 mg
Fat	21.7 g
Fiber	5.2 g
Protein	15.7 g
Sodium	625 mg

* Percent Daily Values are based on a 2,000 calorie diet.

CHICKEN, MONTEREY, BASIL PESTO PANINI

Ingredients

- 1 focaccia bread, quartered
- 1/2 C. prepared basil pesto
- 1 C. diced cooked chicken
- 1/2 C. diced green bell pepper
- 1/4 C. diced red onion
- 1 C. shredded Monterey Jack cheese

Directions

- Heat up your Panini grill according to the instruction of the manufacturer.
- Spread pesto over each half of focaccia bread before putting chicken, cheese, bell pepper and onion over the lower half, and closing it up to make a sandwich.
- Cook this Panini in the preheated grill for about 5 minutes or until the outside is golden brown.

Serving: 4

Timing Information:

Preparation	Cooking	Total Time
15 mins	5 mins	20 mins

Nutritional Information:

Calories	641 kcal
Carbohydrates	60.9 g
Cholesterol	61 mg
Fat	29.4 g
Fiber	4.4 g
Protein	32.4 g
Sodium	1076 mg

* Percent Daily Values are based on a 2,000 calorie diet.

CHEDDAR, CHIPOTLE, CAESAR, BACON PANINI

Ingredients

- 2 slices sourdough bread
- 1/4 C. Caesar salad dressing
- 1 cooked chicken breast, diced
- 1/2 C. shredded Cheddar cheese
- 1 tbsp bacon bits
- 1 1/2 tsps chipotle chili powder, or to taste
- 2 tbsps softened butter

Directions

- Heat up your Panini grill according to the instruction of the manufacturer.
- Spread Caesar dressing over each half of the bread before putting chicken, cheddar cheese, bacon bits and chipotle chili powder over the lower half, and closing it up to make a sandwich.
- Put some butter on top and cook this Panini in the preheated grill for about 4 minutes or until the outside is golden brown.

Serving: 1

Timing Information:

Preparation	Cooking	Total Time
10 mins	5 mins	15 mins

Nutritional Information:

Calories	1243 kcal
Carbohydrates	31.9 g
Cholesterol	312 mg
Fat	83.9 g
Fiber	1.5 g
Protein	85.7 g
Sodium	1813 mg

* Percent Daily Values are based on a 2,000 calorie diet.

ROMANO, BASIL, CHICKEN, CAESAR PANINI

Ingredients

- 1/4 C. packed fresh basil leaves
- 1/4 C. olive oil
- 4 cloves garlic, diced
- 2 tbsps grated Romano cheese
- 1 tsp dried oregano
- 1 tsp ground black pepper
- 2 skinless, boneless chicken breast halves
- 2 tbsps creamy Caesar salad dressing
- 6 slices Italian bread with sesame seeds (Scali)
- 1/2 C. shredded iceberg lettuce
- 2 thin slices smoked mozzarella

Directions

- Heat up your grill and put some oil on the grate
- Blend a mixture of basil, oregano, oil, garlic, Romano cheese and pepper in a blender until smooth.
- Now grill chicken on the preheated grill for about 5 minutes each side.
- Spread Caesar dressing over the bread and put lettuce before putting additional slice of bread over it.
- Now put cooked chicken breast and smoked mozzarella before closing it up to make a sandwich.
- Cook this Panini in the preheated grill for about three minutes or until the outside is golden brown.

Serving: 2

Timing Information:

Preparation	Cooking	Total Time
20 mins	16 mins	36 mins

Nutritional Information:

Calories	587 kcal
Carbohydrates	20 g
Cholesterol	85 mg
Fat	41.5 g
Fiber	1.8 g
Protein	32.5 g
Sodium	523 mg

* Percent Daily Values are based on a 2,000 calorie diet.

SOURDOUGH, PROVOLONE, PESTO PANINI

Ingredients

- 1/2 C. Extra Virgin Olive Oil
- 8 slices sourdough bread
- 1/4 C. pesto
- 16 thin slices Provolone cheese
- 12 thin slices prosciutto
- 4 whole, roasted red peppers, julienned

Directions

- Heat up your Panini grill according to the instruction of the manufacturer.
- Spread pesto over each half of the bread before putting ½ of cheese, prosciutto, pepper strips and the remaining cheese over the lower half, and closing it up to make a sandwich.
- Put some butter on top and cook this Panini in the preheated grill for about 4 minutes or until the outside is golden brown.

Serving: 4

Timing Information:

Preparation	Cooking	Total Time
15 mins	4 mins	19 mins

Nutritional Information:

Calories	798 kcal
Carbohydrates	27.4 g
Cholesterol	76 mg
Fat	63.9 g
Fiber	2.1 g
Protein	31 g
Sodium	1754 mg

* Percent Daily Values are based on a 2,000 calorie diet.

Avocado, Turkey, Spinach, Ciabatta

Ingredients

- 4 slices artisan bread such as ciabatta
- 2 tsps honey Dijon salad dressing
- 1/2 C. baby spinach leaves
- 1/4 lb sliced oven-roasted deli turkey breast
- 1/4 red onion, cut into strips
- 1 ripe avocado from Mexico, peeled, pitted and thickly sliced
- Salt and pepper to taste
- 1/4 C. crumbled soft goat cheese
- Non-stick cooking spray

Directions

- Heat up your Panini grill according to the instruction of the manufacturer.
- Spread honey Dijon dressing, spinach leaves, turkey breast and red onion over lower half of the bread before putting avocado slices, salt, pepper and goat cheese over the upper half, and closing it up to make a sandwich.
- Put some butter on top and cook this Panini in the preheated grill for about 8 minutes or until the outside is golden brown.

Serving: 2

Timing Information:

Preparation	Cooking	Total Time
10 mins	10 mins	20 mins

Nutritional Information:

Calories	469 kcal
Carbohydrates	45.5 g
Cholesterol	37 mg
Fat	23.8 g
Fiber	8.5 g
Protein	22.1 g
Sodium	1250 mg

* Percent Daily Values are based on a 2,000 calorie diet.

Mushroom, Salami, Ham, Provolone Panini

Ingredients

- 1 tsp butter
- 2 tbsps sliced fresh mushrooms
- 1/2 C. tomato sauce
- 4 ciabatta rolls, split
- 2 cloves garlic, diced
- 1 tbsp dried oregano
- 8 slices hot Genoa salami
- 8 slices roasted ham
- 2 tbsps diced red onion
- 2 tbsps chopped roasted red pepper
- 2 tbsps chopped black olives
- 4 leaves basil, chopped
- 4 slices provolone cheese

Directions

- Heat up your Panini grill according to the instruction of the manufacturer.
- Cook mushrooms in hot butter for about seven minutes.
- Spread tomato sauce, garlic, oregano, salami slices, two slices of ham, red onion, basil, mushrooms, olives, red pepper and put provolone cheese in the very end over the lower half of the bread before closing it up to make a sandwich.
- Cook this Panini in the preheated grill for about 5 minutes or until the outside is golden brown.

Serving: 4

Timing Information:

Preparation	Cooking	Total Time
20 mins	5 mins	25 mins

Nutritional Information:

Calories	652 kcal
Carbohydrates	36.9 g
Cholesterol	111 mg
Fat	38.9 g
Fiber	2.9 g
Protein	37.1 g
Sodium	2696 mg

* Percent Daily Values are based on a 2,000 calorie diet.

THE BEST PANINI DIP

Ingredients

- 1 tbsp mayonnaise
- 1 1/2 tsps hot pepper sauce
- 2 tsps garlic powder

Directions

- Combine all the ingredients very thoroughly in a bowl before refrigerating it for at least an hour.
- Serve with any Panini.

Serving: 1

Timing Information:

Preparation	Cooking	Total Time
5 mins		5 mins

Nutritional Information:

Calories	118 kcal
Carbohydrates	4.6 g
Cholesterol	5 mg
Fat	11 g
Fiber	0.6 g
Protein	1.1 g
Sodium	265 mg

* Percent Daily Values are based on a 2,000 calorie diet.

Yogurt, Parmesan, Basil, Turkey Panini

Ingredients

- 3 tbsps reduced-fat mayonnaise
- 2 tbsps nonfat plain yogurt
- 2 tbsps shredded Parmesan cheese
- 2 tbsps chopped fresh basil
- 1 tsp lemon juice
- Freshly ground pepper to taste
- 8 slices whole-wheat bread
- 8 oz thinly sliced reduced-sodium deli turkey
- 8 tomato slices
- 2 tsps canola oil

Directions

- Heat up your Panini grill according to the instruction of the manufacturer.
- Spread a mixture of mayonnaise, lemon juice, yogurt, Parmesan, basil and pepper over each half of the bread before putting turkey and tomato slices over the lower half, and closing it up to make a sandwich.
- Put some butter on top and cook this Panini in the preheated grill for about 4 minutes or until the outside is golden brown.

Serving: 4

Timing Information:

Preparation	Cooking	Total Time
15 mins	10 mins	25 mins

Nutritional Information:

Calories	279 kcal
Carbohydrates	26.9 g
Cholesterol	31 mg
Fat	9.7 g
Fiber	4.4 g
Protein	22.1 g
Sodium	673 mg

* Percent Daily Values are based on a 2,000 calorie diet.

CASHEWS, CHICKPEAS, AND MUSHROOMS BROWN RICE (PILAF I)

Ingredients

- 1 1/2 C. water
- 1/2 tsp salt
- 3/4 C. uncooked brown rice
- 3 tbsps butter
- 1 1/2 C. chopped onion
- 1 clove garlic, minced
- 2 carrots, sliced
- 2 C. fresh sliced mushrooms
- 1 C. chickpeas
- 2 eggs, beaten
- freshly ground black pepper
- 1/4 C. chopped fresh parsley
- 1/4 C. chopped cashews

Directions

- Boil your rice in 1.5 C. of water for 47 mins, in a covered pot over low heat.
- Halfway through the rice's cooking time, begin to stir fry your onions in butter until tender then combine in: carrots and garlic and fry for 6 more mins.
- Add the mushrooms and cook for 11 mins before adding the chickpeas and frying for 2 more mins.
- Cook your eggs in a pan after the rice is done and then add to them: nuts, parsley, and pepper.
- Combine the rice with the eggs and also the veggies.
- Serve everything topped with some soy sauce. Enjoy.

Amount per serving (4 total)

Timing Information:

Preparation	10 m
Cooking	1 h
Total Time	1 h 20 m

Nutritional Information:

Calories	409 kcal
Fat	17.1 g
Carbohydrates	54g
Protein	12.5 g
Cholesterol	116 mg
Sodium	653 mg

* Percent Daily Values are based on a 2,000 calorie diet.

BUTTERY AND BAKED BROWN RICE

Ingredients

- 1 1/2 C. brown rice
- 1 tsp salt
- 2 tbsps butter
- 3 C. boiling water

Directions

- Get your water boiling then set your oven to 400 degrees before doing anything else.
- Now get a baking dish and add to it: butter, salt, and rice.
- Top the mix with the boiling water and place a covering of foil over the dish.
- Cook everything in the oven for 1 hr, then stir it.
- Enjoy.

Amount per serving (6 total)

Timing Information:

Preparation	10 m
Cooking	1 h
Total Time	1 h 10 m

Nutritional Information:

Calories	206 kcal
Fat	5.1 g
Carbohydrates	36.2g
Protein	3.6 g
Cholesterol	10 mg
Sodium	420 mg

* Percent Daily Values are based on a 2,000 calorie diet.

INSTANT LEMON AND PARSLEY BROWN RICE

Ingredients

- 1 C. instant brown rice (such as Minute(R))
- 1/2 tsp dried parsley
- 1/4 tsp ground black pepper (optional)
- 1 tbsp unsalted butter
- 1/2 tsp lemon juice
- 7 fluid oz. low-sodium chicken broth, or more if needed

Directions

- Get a measuring cup and add in: lemon juice, butter, and 7 oz. of broth.
- Everything should equal exactly one 1 C.
- Now get a bowl, add in: black pepper, the broth mix, parsley, and rice.
- Place a lid on the bowl and cook it in the microwave for 8 mins.
- Now remove the lid and let it cool for 7 mins before stirring.
- Enjoy.

Amount per serving (4 total)

Timing Information:

Preparation	10 m
Cooking	10 m
Total Time	20 m

Nutritional Information:

Calories	109 kcal
Fat	3.6 g
Carbohydrates	16.8g
Protein	2.5 g
Cholesterol	8 mg
Sodium	24 mg

* Percent Daily Values are based on a 2,000 calorie diet.

PEPPER, BALSAMIC, DIJON, AND RAISIN BROWN RICE (SALAD I)

Ingredients

- 1 1/2 C. uncooked brown rice
- 3 C. water
- 1 red bell pepper, thinly sliced
- 1 C. frozen green peas, thawed
- 1/2 C. raisins
- 1/4 sweet onion (such as Vidalia(R)), chopped
- 1/4 C. chopped Kalamata olives
- 1/2 C. vegetable oil
- 1/4 C. balsamic vinegar
- 1 1/4 tsps Dijon mustard
- salt and ground black pepper to taste
- 1/4 C. feta cheese

Directions

- Get your water and rice boiling, place a lid on the pot, set the heat to low, and let the contents cook, with a low heat, for 47 mins.
- Get a bowl, mix: olives, bell pepper, onions, raisins, and peas.
- Get a 2nd bowl, combine: mustard, vinegar, and veggie oil.
- Combine both bowls then add in your ice and add some pepper and salt before adding in some cheese. Enjoy.

Amount per serving (6 total)

Timing Information:

Preparation	15 m
Cooking	45 m
Total Time	1 h

Nutritional Information:

Calories	451 kcal
Fat	23.5 g
Carbohydrates	54.6g
Protein	7.1 g
Cholesterol	9 mg
Sodium	338 mg

* Percent Daily Values are based on a 2,000 calorie diet.

Peppers, Onions, and Cheddar Brown Rice

Ingredients

- 2 C. water
- 1 C. brown rice
- 1/2 red bell peppers, seeded and chopped
- 1/4 red onion, chopped
- 1 C. shredded low-fat Cheddar cheese

Directions

- Get your water and rice boiling before placing a lid on the pot, setting the heat to low, and letting the contents cook for 47 mins.
- Stir fry your onions and peppers in nonstick spray, until brown, and combine them with the rice, when it is finished.
- Combine in your cheese and let it melt before plating the dish.
- Enjoy.

Amount per serving (8 total)

Timing Information:

Preparation	10 m
Cooking	45 m
Total Time	55 m

Nutritional Information:

Calories	95 kcal
Fat	1.5 g
Carbohydrates	15g
Protein	4.9 g
Cholesterol	3 mg
Sodium	87 mg

* Percent Daily Values are based on a 2,000 calorie diet.

EASY LATIN STYLE BROWN RICE

Ingredients

- 1 (14 oz.) can chicken broth
- 1 (15 oz.) can diced tomatoes with green chili peppers
- 1 tsp salt
- 1 C. brown rice

Directions

- Boil: rice, broth, salt, and tomatoes.
- Once everything is boiling place a lid on the pot, set the heat to low, and cook the contents for 1 hr.
- Let the rice cool for 7 mins before stirring it.
- Enjoy.

Amount per serving (4 total)

Timing Information:

Preparation	10 m
Cooking	1 h
Total Time	1 h 10 m

Nutritional Information:

Calories	156 kcal
Fat	1.3 g
Carbohydrates	32.3g
Protein	4 g
Cholesterol	2 mg
Sodium	1479 mg

* Percent Daily Values are based on a 2,000 calorie diet.

Brown Rice Risotto I

Ingredients

- 1 quart vegetable broth, or as needed
- 5 C. water, or as needed
- 1/2 lb asparagus, cut into 2-inch pieces
- 2 tbsps olive oil
- 1 C. finely chopped onion
- 2 cloves garlic, finely chopped
- 2 C. short-grain brown rice
- 2 carrots, peeled and diced
- 2 zucchini, diced
- 1/2 C. green peas, thawed if frozen
- 2/3 C. grated Parmesan cheese
- 1 tbsp butter
- salt and ground black pepper to taste

Directions

- Boil your water and broth then add the asparagus to it and cook for 4 mins.
- Place the veggies to the side in some cold water for 7 mins.
- Now remove all the liquid from the bowl, place a lid on the boiling broth, and let it continue to boil.
- Stir fry your garlic and onions in olive oil for 7 mins then add the rice and cook for 6 more mins.
- Now add a half a C., at a time, of the hot broth, to the rice and stir until it is basically absorbed by the rice.
- Continue doing this for about 20 mins.

- Add in the carrots and continue adding liquid in batches for 20 more mins.
- Now add in the zucchini, peas, and asparagus.
- Cook everything for 5 more mins then combine in the butter and parmesan.
- Once everything has melted add some pepper and salt and add .5 C. of broth as well.
- Enjoy.

Amount per serving (6 total)

Timing Information:

Preparation	30 m
Cooking	1 h
Total Time	1 h 30 m

Nutritional Information:

Calories	322 kcal
Fat	10.7 g
Carbohydrates	47.1g
Protein	10 g
Cholesterol	13 mg
Sodium	500 mg

* Percent Daily Values are based on a 2,000 calorie diet.

Zucchini, Chicken, Mushrooms, and Swiss Brown Rice

Ingredients

- 1/3 C. brown rice
- 1 C. vegetable broth
- 1 tbsp olive oil
- 1/3 C. diced onion
- 1 medium zucchini, thinly sliced
- 2 cooked skinless boneless chicken breast halves, chopped
- 1/2 C. sliced mushrooms
- 1/2 tsp cumin
- salt to taste
- ground cayenne pepper to taste
- 1 (15 oz.) can black beans, drained
- 1 (4 oz.) can diced green chile peppers, drained
- 1/3 C. shredded carrots
- 2 C. shredded Swiss cheese

Directions

- Boil your broth and veggies, once everything is boiling place a lid on the pot, set the heat to low, and let the contents gently cook for 47 mins.
- Coat a baking dish with oil and then set your oven to 350 degrees before doing anything else.
- Stir fry your onions, until soft, in olive oil, for about 7 mins, then combine in: mushrooms, zucchini, and chicken along with some cayenne, cumin, and salt.
- Stir fry the mix until the chicken is fully done.

- Get a bowl, combine: half of the cheese, the rice, carrots, onions, chilies, zucchini, chilies, chicken, beans, and mushrooms.
- Pour all the contents into the baking dish and cook it all in the oven covered with foil for 32 mins then take off the foil and cook for 8 more mins.
- Let the casserole stand for 10 mins before plating.
- Enjoy.

Amount per serving (8 total)

Timing Information:

Preparation	15 m
Cooking	1 h 35 m
Total Time	1 h 50 m

Nutritional Information:

Calories	337 kcal
Fat	21 g
Carbohydrates	11.5g
Protein	25.3 g
Cholesterol	77 mg
Sodium	363 mg

* Percent Daily Values are based on a 2,000 calorie diet.

MEATY NO-MEAT BROWN RICE BAKE BROWN RICE

Ingredients

- 1 C. brown rice
- 1 C. beef broth
- 1 (14.5 oz.) can chicken broth
- 1/4 C. butter, melted
- 1 tsp garlic salt
- 1 tsp seasoned salt

Directions

- Set your oven to 350 degrees before doing anything else.
- Get a baking dish and layer in it: rice, both broths, and butter.
- Top with: seasoned salt and garlic salt.
- Cook everything in the oven for 1 hr.
- Enjoy.

Amount per serving (8 total)

Timing Information:

Preparation	10 m
Cooking	1 h
Total Time	1 h 10 m

Nutritional Information:

Calories	140 kcal
Fat	6.5 g
Carbohydrates	18.3g
Protein	2.2 g
Cholesterol	15 mg
Sodium	482 mg

* Percent Daily Values are based on a 2,000 calorie diet.

Easy Louisiana Style Brown Rice

Ingredients

- 2 tbsps butter
- 8 oz. andouille sausage, cut into 1/4-inch slices
- 2 tbsps ground paprika
- 1 tbsp ground cumin
- 1/2 tsp cayenne pepper
- 1/2 C. diced tomatoes
- 1 large green bell pepper, diced
- 2 stalks celery, sliced 1/4 inch thick
- 4 green onions, thinly sliced
- 1 tsp salt
- 1 bay leaf
- 1 C. uncooked brown rice
- 3 C. chicken stock
- 1 lb large shrimp, peeled and deveined
- salt and ground black pepper to taste

Directions

- Stir fry your sausage in butter, in a big pot, until browned.
- Then add in: cayenne, cumin, and paprika. Cook for 2 more mins.
- Now combine in: salt, bay leaf, tomatoes, onions, pepper, and celery.
- Stir the contents and cook for 1 more min before adding the stock and rice.
- Get everything boiling and once it is boiling place a lid on the pot, set the heat to low, and let the contents cook for 47 mins.
- Add in the shrimp and let them cook for 7 mins before adding in some pepper and salt. Enjoy.

Amount per serving (4 total)

Timing Information:

Preparation	15 m
Cooking	1 h
Total Time	1 h 15 m

Nutritional Information:

Calories	495 kcal
Fat	25.2 g
Carbohydrates	37.3g
Protein	30.3 g
Cholesterol	221 mg
Sodium	1909 mg

* Percent Daily Values are based on a 2,000 calorie diet.

EASY MEXICAN STYLE BROWN RICE

Ingredients

- 2 C. cooked brown rice
- 1 (15 oz.) can kidney beans, rinsed and drained
- 1 (15 oz.) can black beans, rinsed and drained
- 1 (15.25 oz.) can whole kernel corn, drained
- 1 small onion, diced
- 1 green bell pepper, diced
- 2 jalapeno peppers, seeded and diced
- 1 lime, zested and juiced
- 1/4 C. chopped cilantro leaves
- 1 tsp minced garlic
- 1 1/2 tsps ground cumin
- salt to taste

Directions

- Get a bowl, combine: cumin, rice, garlic, beans, cilantro, corn, lime juice & zest, onions, jalapenos, and green peppers.
- Add in your preferred amount of pepper and salt and place the contents in the fridge for 60 mins then stir everything and serve.
- Enjoy.

Amount per serving (10 total)

Timing Information:

Preparation	
Cooking	20 m
Total Time	1 h 20 m

Nutritional Information:

Calories	124 kcal
Fat	1 g
Carbohydrates	26g
Protein	4.7 g
Cholesterol	0 mg
Sodium	220 mg

* Percent Daily Values are based on a 2,000 calorie diet.

BLACK BEAN AND RICE BURGERS BROWN RICE (VEGETARIAN APPROVED)

Ingredients

- 1/2 C. uncooked brown rice
- 1 C. water
- 2 (16 oz.) cans black beans, rinsed and drained
- 1 green bell pepper, halved and seeded
- 1 onion, quartered
- 1/2 C. sliced mushrooms
- 6 cloves garlic, peeled
- 3/4 C. shredded mozzarella cheese
- 2 eggs
- 1 tbsp chili powder
- 1 tbsp ground cumin
- 1 tbsp garlic salt
- 1 tsp hot sauce
- 1/2 C. dry bread crumbs, or as needed

Directions

- Get your water and rice boiling, then place a lid on the pot, set the heat to low, and let the contents gently cook for 47 mins.
- Heat up your grill and cover the grate with foil.
- With a blender, process: garlic, bell pepper, mushrooms, and onions. Then place everything in a bowl.
- Now blend the mozzarella and the rice and add them to the same bowl
- Get a 2nd bowl, mash: black beans until paste like.

- Then add in the blended mix.
- Get a 3rb bowl, combine: beaten eggs, hot sauce, chili powder, garlic salt, and cumin.
- Add this to the beans and then mix in your bread crumbs.
- Shape the bean mix into 6 burgers then grill each for 7 mins per side.
- Enjoy the patties with sesame seed buns and some mayo.

Amount per serving (6 total)

Timing Information:

Preparation	25 m
Cooking	16 m
Total Time	41 m

Nutritional Information:

Calories	317 kcal
Fat	5.8 g
Carbohydrates	49.4g
Protein	18.2 g
Cholesterol	71 mg
Sodium	1704 mg

* Percent Daily Values are based on a 2,000 calorie diet.

Walnuts, Broccoli, and Cheddar Brown Rice

Ingredients

- 1/2 C. chopped walnuts
- 1 tbsp butter
- 1 onion, chopped
- 1/2 tsp minced garlic
- 1 C. uncooked instant brown rice
- 1 C. vegetable broth
- 1 lb fresh broccoli florets
- 1/2 tsp salt
- 1/8 tsp ground black pepper
- 1 C. shredded Cheddar cheese

Directions

- Set your oven to 350 degrees before doing anything else.
- Get a baking dish and toast your nuts in the oven for 9 mins.
- Microwave the broccoli until soft, then add in some pepper and salt.
- Now stir fry your garlic and onions in butter for 4 mins then add in the broth and rice. Get everything boiling, then place a lid on the pot, and let the contents, gently cook over a lower level of heat for 9 mins.
- On each serving plate add a layer of rice, then some broccoli, then nuts, and finally some cheese.
- Enjoy.

Amount per serving (4 total)

Timing Information:

Preparation	15 m
Cooking	25 m
Total Time	40 m

Nutritional Information:

Calories	368 kcal
Fat	22.9 g
Carbohydrates	30.4g
Protein	15.1 g
Cholesterol	37 mg
Sodium	643 mg

* Percent Daily Values are based on a 2,000 calorie diet.

Mandarin Chicken

Ingredients

- 1 C. orange juice
- 1 tbsp soy sauce
- 1 (1 oz.) envelope dry onion soup mix
- 1/2 tsp garlic powder, or to taste
- 8 chicken thighs

Directions

- Set your oven to 350 degrees before doing anything else.
- Get a bowl, combine: garlic powder, orange juice, onion soup, and soy sauce.
- Clean your chicken under fresh cold water then enter them into a casserole dish.
- Top the chicken pieces with the onion soup mix.
- Now cook everything in the oven for 90 mins.
- Baste the chicken every 20 mins.
- Enjoy.

Amount per serving (8 total)

Timing Information:

Preparation	5 m
Cooking	1 h 30 m
Total Time	1 h 35 m

Nutritional Information:

Calories	180 kcal
Fat	9.9 g
Carbohydrates	5.7g
Protein	16.4 g
Cholesterol	59 mg
Sodium	475 mg

* Percent Daily Values are based on a 2,000 calorie diet.

HONEY AND SRIRACHA CHICKEN

Ingredients

- 1/2 C. rice vinegar
- 5 tbsps honey
- 1/3 C. soy sauce (such as Silver Swan(R))
- 1/4 C. Asian (toasted) sesame oil
- 3 tbsps Sriracha
- 3 tbsps minced garlic
- salt to taste
- 8 skinless, boneless chicken thighs
- 1 tbsp chopped green onion (optional)

Directions

- Get a bowl, combine: salt, vinegar, garlic, honey, sriracha, soy sauce, and sesame oil. Divide the sauce amongst two bowls.
- Put your chicken pieces into one of the bowls, then evenly coat them with sauce, and place them in the fridge, with a covering of plastic, for 60 mins.
- Set your oven to 425 degrees before doing anything else.
- Now a get a pan and boil the remaining half of the marinade for 4 mins while stirring. Now put your chicken in a casserole dish and top with one third of the sauce in the pan.
- Cook everything in the oven for 35 mins and baste every 10 mins.
- Let the chicken sit for 15 mins while you get your sauce heated again. Once it is hot again top the chicken with the rest of the hot sauce. Enjoy.

Amount per serving (4 total)

Timing Information:

Preparation	5 m
Cooking	30 m
Total Time	1 h 40 m

Nutritional Information:

Calories	544 kcal
Fat	30.2 g
Carbohydrates	26.6g
Protein	40.6 g
Cholesterol	142 mg
Sodium	1814 mg

* Percent Daily Values are based on a 2,000 calorie diet.

Syrup and Sriracha Chicken

Ingredients

- 1 clove garlic, sliced, or more to taste
- 2 tsps Asian chili pepper sauce, sriracha
- 1 1/2 tbsps maple syrup
- 2 tbsps soy sauce
- 2 tbsps mayonnaise
- 3 tbsps rice vinegar
- salt and freshly ground black pepper to taste
- 2 lbs skinless, boneless chicken thighs
- 1 lime, cut into 8 wedges

Directions

- Place your garlic in a bowl and mash it until pasty.
- Then add in: vinegar, chili pepper sauce, mayo, syrup, and soy sauce.
- Place your chicken thighs in a casserole dish and top them with the garlic sauce.
- Place some plastic around the dish and chill everything it in the fridge for 3 hours.
- Then add some salt to it.
- Grill your chicken pieces for 4 mins per side.
- Then continue cooking for about 8 more mins flipping the chicken every 2 or 3 mins.
- Garnish your chicken with lime wedges. Enjoy.

Amount per serving (8 total)

Timing Information:

Preparation	15 m
Cooking	20 m
Total Time	3 h 40 m

Nutritional Information:

Calories	194 kcal
Fat	10.8 g
Carbohydrates	4g
Protein	19.5 g
Cholesterol	71 mg
Sodium	311 mg

* Percent Daily Values are based on a 2,000 calorie diet.

CREAMY MUSHROOMS AND ONIONS CHICKEN

Ingredients

- 8 chicken thighs
- 1 tbsp vegetable oil
- 1 pinch ground black pepper
- 1 pinch salt
- 1 pinch paprika
- 1 (10.75 oz.) can condensed cream of mushroom soup
- 1 (1 oz.) package dry onion soup mix
- 1 C. sour cream
- 1 tbsp lemon juice
- 1 tsp dried dill weed

Directions

- Get a frying and pan and with some hot oil brown the chicken all over.
- Then add everything to a casserole dish and top with paprika, pepper, and salt.
- Get a bowl, combine: dill, mushroom soup, lemon juice, onion soup, and sour cream.
- Combine everything until smooth and evenly top your chicken with this mix.
- Cook the contents in the oven for 60 mins.
- Enjoy.

Amount per serving (4 total)

Timing Information:

Preparation	10 m
Cooking	1 h
Total Time	1 h 20 m

Nutritional Information:

Calories	637 kcal
Fat	48.8 g
Carbohydrates	12.7g
Protein	36.1 g
Cholesterol	183 mg
Sodium	1284 mg

* Percent Daily Values are based on a 2,000 calorie diet.

French Style and Apricots Chicken

Ingredients

- 12 chicken thighs
- 1 C. apricot preserves
- 1 C. French dressing
- 1 (1 oz.) package dry onion soup mix

Directions

- Set your oven to 350 degrees before doing anything else.
- Get a bowl, combine: soup, apricots, and dressing.
- Get a casserole dish and place your chicken in it then top with the apricot mix.
- Cook everything in the oven for 1 h.
- Enjoy.

Amount per serving (12 total)

Timing Information:

Preparation	10 m
Cooking	1 h
Total Time	1 h 20 m

Nutritional Information:

Calories	342 kcal
Fat	20.1 g
Carbohydrates	23.3g
Protein	15.9 g
Cholesterol	59 mg
Sodium	444 mg

* Percent Daily Values are based on a 2,000 calorie diet.

Dijon, Brown Sugar, and Cayenne Chicken

Ingredients

- 8 large bone-in, skin-on chicken thighs
- 1/2 C. Dijon mustard
- 1/4 C. packed brown sugar
- 1/4 C. red wine vinegar
- 1 tsp dry mustard powder
- 1 tsp salt
- 1 tsp freshly ground black pepper
- 1/2 tsp ground dried chipotle pepper
- 1 pinch cayenne pepper, or to taste
- 4 cloves garlic, minced
- 1 onion, sliced into rings
- 2 tsps vegetable oil, or as needed

Directions

- Get a bowl, combine: cayenne, Dijon, chipotle, vinegar, black pepper, mustard powder, and salt.
- Take your chicken and cut some incisions in them (at least 2). Then place everything in the bowl.
- Place a covering of plastic around the bowl, and put everything in the fridge for 5 to 8 hrs.

- Cover a casserole dish with foil and then set your oven to 450 degrees before doing anything else.
- Pour your onions around the dish and then layer the chicken on top.
- Coat everything with some veggies and top the contents with some cayenne and salt.
- Cook everything in the oven for 50 mins.
- Then plate the chicken.
- Now boil the drippings for 5 mins while stirring.
- Finally top the chicken and onions with the sauce.
- Enjoy.

Amount per serving (8 total)

Timing Information:

Preparation	20 m
Cooking	40 m
Total Time	5 h

Nutritional Information:

Calories	352 kcal
Fat	19 g
Carbohydrates	13.8g
Protein	29.1 g
Cholesterol	106 mg
Sodium	765 mg

* Percent Daily Values are based on a 2,000 calorie diet.

Chicken Thighs VII
(Onions, Carrots, and Rosemary)

Ingredients

- 6 chicken thighs
- salt and ground black pepper to taste
- 1 yellow onion, diced
- 1/4 C. chopped fresh basil, or to taste
- 3 cloves garlic, sliced
- 2 tsps finely chopped fresh rosemary
- 1 1/2 C. chicken broth
- 3 C. diced carrots

Directions

- Set your oven to 375 degrees before doing anything else.
- Place your chicken in a casserole dish and then top everything with: rosemary, basil, garlic, carrots, pepper, salt, and onions.
- Now cover everything in the broth.
- Wrap some foil around the top of the casserole dish and cook the contents in the oven for 65 mins.
- After 65 mins has elapsed remove the covering on the dish and continue cooking for 10 more mins.
- Enjoy.

Amount per serving (6 total)

Timing Information:

Preparation	15 m
Cooking	1 h 10 m
Total Time	1 h 25 m

Nutritional Information:

Calories	238 kcal
Fat	12.2 g
Carbohydrates	10.8g
Protein	20.6 g
Cholesterol	72 mg
Sodium	352 mg

* Percent Daily Values are based on a 2,000 calorie diet.

THANKS FOR READING! NOW LET'S TRY SOME **SUSHI** AND **DUMP DINNERS**....

http://bit.ly/2443TFg

To grab this **box set** simply follow the link mentioned above, or tap the book cover.

This will take you to a page where you can simply enter your email address and a PDF version of the **box set** will be emailed to you.

I hope you are ready for some serious cooking!

http://bit.ly/2443TFg

You will also receive updates about all my new books when they are free.

Also don't forget to like and subscribe on the social networks. I love meeting my readers. Links to all my profiles are below so please click and connect :)

Facebook

Twitter

Come On...
Let's Be Friends :)

I adore my readers and love connecting with them socially. Please follow the links below so we can connect on Facebook, Twitter, and Google+.

Facebook

Twitter

I also have a blog that I regularly update for my readers so check it out below.

My Blog

Can I Ask A Favour?

If you found this book interesting, or have otherwise found any benefit in it. Then may I ask that you post a review of it on Amazon? Nothing excites me more than new reviews, especially reviews which suggest new topics for writing. I do read all reviews and I always factor feedback into my newer works.

So if you are willing to take ten minutes to write what you sincerely thought about this book then please visit our Amazon page and post your opinions.

Again thank you!

INTERESTED IN OTHER EASY COOKBOOKS?

Everything is easy! Check out my Amazon Author page for more great cookbooks:

For a complete listing of all my books please see my author page.

Made in the USA
Coppell, TX
16 March 2022

75067718R00085